Read for a
Better World™

BIG RIGS
A First Look

PERCY LEED

GRL Consultant, Diane Craig, Certified Literacy Specialist

Lerner Publications ◆ Minneapolis

TABLE OF CONTENTS

Big Rigs 4

You Connect! 21

STEM Snapshot 22

Photo Glossary 23

Learn More 23

Index. 24

Big Rigs

A big rig is a kind of truck.

tractor

trailer

It carries goods
like food and toys.
It has a tractor.
It has a trailer.

cab

The tractor is in front.
It has the cab.

The driver sits there.

The trailer
holds the goods.
The tractor pulls it.

What goods can fit
in a big rig?

Big rigs have
many wheels.

Big rigs are very heavy.
They are as long as
two school buses.

Drivers need training to drive big rigs.

Why do big rig drivers need training?

Some drivers
must go very far.
They drive for many
days or weeks.

Their cabs have beds.

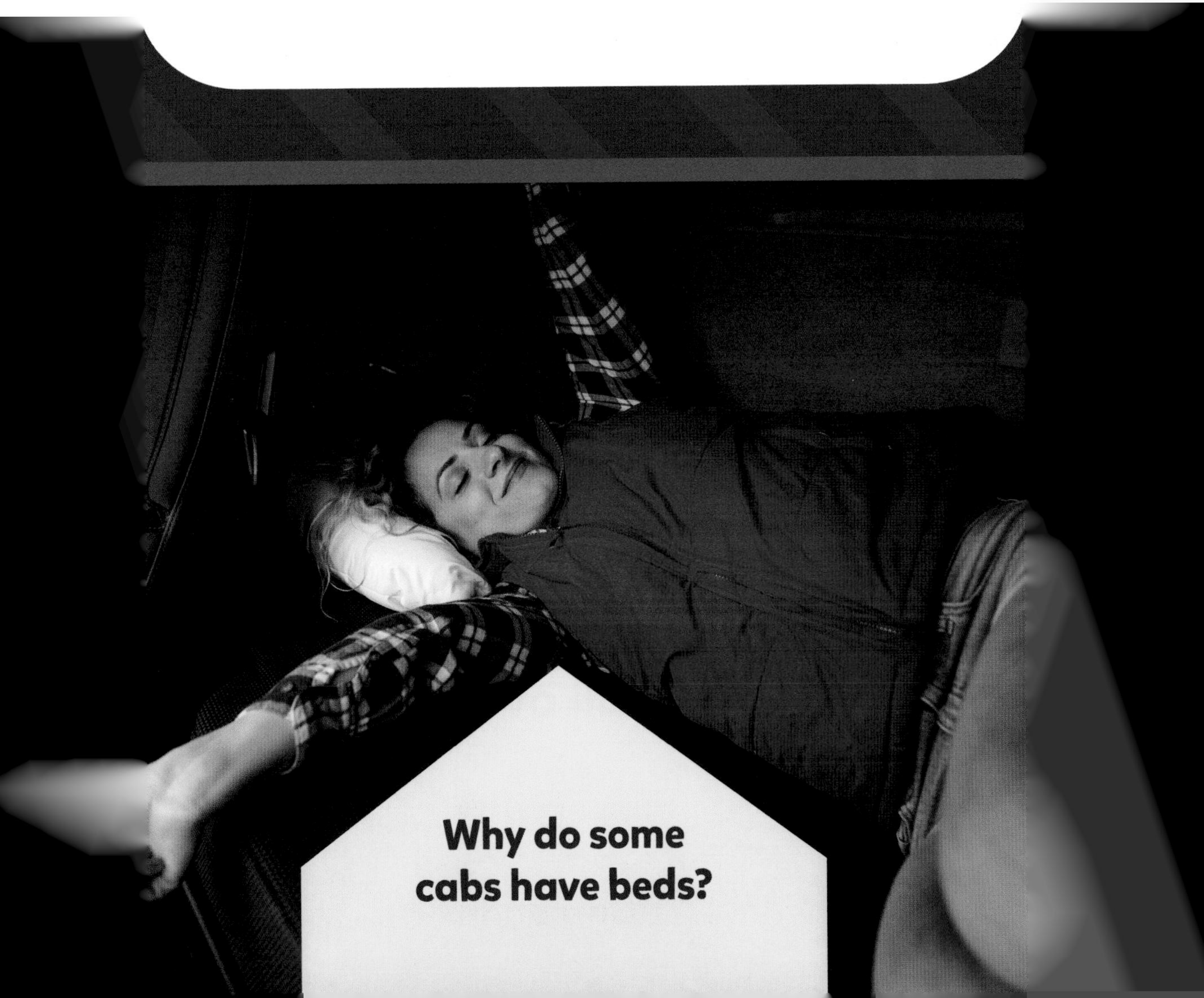

Why do some cabs have beds?

Big rigs go all over.

You Connect!

Have you ever seen a big rig?

Would you want to drive
a big rig?

How can you learn more
about big rigs?

STEM Snapshot

Encourage students to think and ask questions like scientists. Ask the reader:

What is something you learned about big rigs?

What is something you noticed about big rig parts?

What is something you still want to learn about big rigs?

Photo Glossary

cab

tractor

trailer

wheel

Learn More

Allan, John. *Let's Look at Trucks and Tractors*. Minneapolis: Hungry Tomato, 2019.

Freels, Korynn. *Ripley Readers Trucks!* Orlando: Ripley Publishing, 2019.

Rathburn, Betsy. *Truck Drivers*. Minneapolis: Bellwether Media, 2020.

Index

cab, 8, 19

driver, 9, 16, 17, 18

goods, 7, 10, 11

tractor, 7, 8, 10

trailer, 7, 10

wheels, 12

Photo Acknowledgments

The images in this book are used with the permission of: © imagedepotpro/iStockphoto, pp. 4–5; © Joey Ingelhart/iStockphoto, pp. 6–7, 23 (tractor, trailer); © kali9/iStockphoto, pp. 8, 16, 18, 23 (cab); © xavierarnau/iStockphoto, p. 9; © deadandliving/iStockphoto, pp. 10–11; © Stefonlinton/iStockphoto, pp. 12–13, 23 (wheel); © Sundry Photography/iStockphoto, pp. 14–15; © shaunl/iStockphoto, pp. 15, 20; © gk-6mt/iStockphoto, pp. 16–17; © Smederevac/iStockphoto, p. 19.

Cover Photograph: © Andyqwe/iStockphoto

Design Elements: © Mighty Media, Inc.

Lerner Publications Company
An imprint of Lerner Publishing Group, Inc.
241 First Avenue North
Minneapolis, MN 55401 USA

For reading levels and more information, look up this title at www.lernerbooks.com.

Main body text set in Mikado a Medium.
Typeface provided by Hannes von Doehren.

Library of Congress Cataloging-in-Publication Data

Names: Leed, Percy, 1968–author.
Title: Big rigs : a first look / Percy Leed.
Description: Minneapolis : Lerner Publications, [2024] | Series: Read about vehicles (Read for a better world) | Includes bibliographical references and index. | Audience: Ages 5–8 | Audience: Grades K–1 | Summary: "Big rigs can have eighteen wheels, sometimes more! With all the goods they carry around, they have to be big. Full-color photographs and leveled text give readers a peek inside these huge vehicles"—Provided by publisher.
Identifiers: LCCN 2022035587 (print) | LCCN 2022035588 (ebook) | ISBN 9781728491394 (library binding) | ISBN 9798765603581 (paperback) | ISBN 9781728499666 (ebook)
Subjects: LCSH: Tractor trailer combinations—Juvenile literature.
Classification: LCC TL230.15 .L44 2023 (print) | LCC TL230.15 (ebook) | DDC 629.224—dc23/eng/20221004

LC record available at https://lccn.loc.gov/2022035587
LC ebook record available at https://lccn.loc.gov/2022035588

Manufactured in the United States of America
1 – CG – 7/15/23